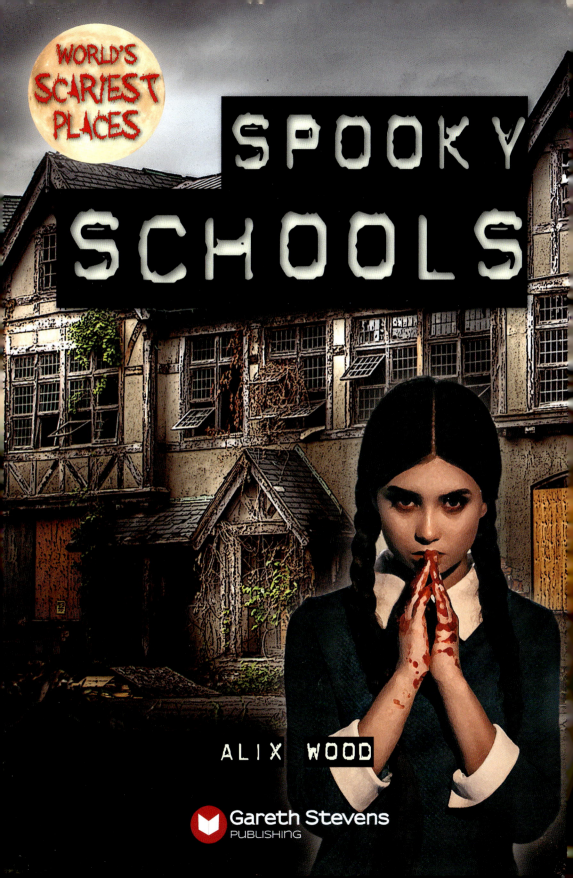

Please visit our website, **www.garethstevens.com**. For a free color catalog of all our high-quality books, call toll free 1-800-542-2595 or fax 1-877-542-2596.

Cataloging-in-Publication Data

Names: Wood, Alix.
Title: Spooky schools / Alix Wood.
Description: New York : Gareth Stevens Publishing, 2020.
| Series: World's scariest places | Includes glossary and index.
Identifiers: ISBN 9781538242490 (pbk.) | ISBN 9781538241974 (library bound) | ISBN 9781538242506 (6 pack)
Subjects: LCSH: Haunted schools--Juvenile literature.
| Haunted places--Juvenile literature.
Classification: LCC BF1478.W64 2020 | DDC 133.1'22--dc23

First Edition

Published in 2020 by
Gareth Stevens Publishing
111 East 14th Street, Suite 349
New York, NY 10003

© Alix Wood Books

Produced for Gareth Stevens by Alix Wood Books
Designed by Alix Wood
Editor: Eloise Macgregor

Photo credits:
Cover, 1, 3, 4, 5, 7, 10 bottom, 12-13, 14, 15, 16 inset, 18, 24, 25, 26, 27, 29 © Adobe Stock Images; 6 © Proper Dave; 8, 9 © Thomas James Caldwell; 11 © Penang State Museum; 12 inset © Philip Howard; 16, 17 © Mary66; 18 background © Antake; 19 bottom © Hyo Lee; 20 © Alice Ramirez, 21 © C. Hanchey; 22 © Harry Penston; 27 inset © Paul Henry; 28 © Joyce Nussbaum; all other images are in the public domain

All rights reserved. No part of this book may be reproduced in any form without permission from the publisher, except by reviewer.

Printed in the United States of America

CPSIA compliance information: Batch #CS19GS. For further information contact Gareth Stevens, New York, New York at 1-800-542-2595.

Contents

Introduction 4
Kangaroo Inn School, Australia 6
Pennhurst State School, Pennsylvania 8
Victoria Institution, Malaysia 10
Dow Hill School, India 12
William Fremd High School, Illinois 14
Mgotjane Primary School, Swaziland 16
Yanagawa High School, Japan 18
El Paso High School, Texas 20
Saint Bathans' School, New Zealand 22
Bristol Tennessee High School, Tennessee . 24
Tat Tak School, Hong Kong 26
Fallsvale Elementary School, California ... 28
Glossary 30
Further Information 31
Index 32

Schools are usually happy places, full of the sound of children playing and laughing. In some schools, though, not everyone who attends is actually alive. Some schools are believed to be haunted by ghosts! Take a look at these terrifying stories of truly scary schools!

1971, Burnley Wood School, England. A janitor was finishing his rounds when he heard a small girl singing. He was about to lock up, so he went searching for the girl. He found her skipping along the corridor, humming to herself. Then she suddenly vanished into thin air!

Other staff also saw the ghostly child running in and out of rooms along the corridor late at night. The school has since been knocked down.

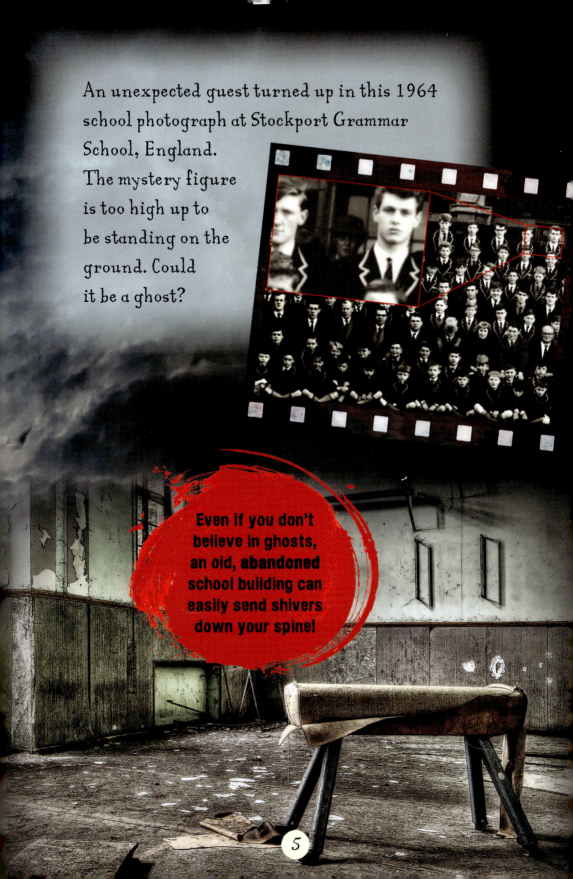

An unexpected guest turned up in this 1964 school photograph at Stockport Grammar School, England. The mystery figure is too high up to be standing on the ground. Could it be a ghost?

Even if you don't believe in ghosts, an old, abandoned school building can easily send shivers down your spine!

Kangaroo Inn School, Australia

In a remote part of Australia, a school was built opposite the ruins of the old Kangaroo Inn. The Inn was a busy stop-off point for people heading for the goldfields during the **gold rush**. People noticed that a young Englishman staying there one night had a lot of money in his wallet. He was found dead with his throat cut the next morning, his wallet and papers missing. His murderer was never caught.

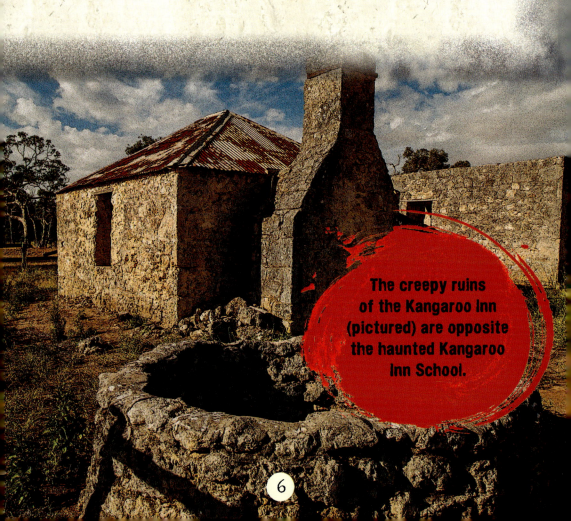

The creepy ruins of the Kangaroo Inn (pictured) are opposite the haunted Kangaroo Inn School.

During an organized school sleepover, students and staff heard a dog barking. Searching the school, they found a small terrier in the corridor. The dog ran through the wall, chasing a glowing green orb. Eventually the dog and the orb floated away.

Legend said that a Chinese couple who ran the Kangaroo Inn were buried under where the school now stands. Several ghostly events have been reported at the school at night. Teachers have experienced being shaken by the shoulders, or feeling suddenly very cold when locking up the school after dark. Could the ghosts of the murdered Englishman, or the dead owners, have come back to haunt the area?

Pennhurst State School, Pennsylvania

This school in Pennsylvania housed and educated young people with mental disabilities and **epilepsy**. Ghosts of the students that attended the school are said to haunt the old buildings today. There were several deaths there over the years, and stories of poor treatment of some students.

In the 1980s, nine staff members were charged with being violent to pupils and allowing pupils to attack each other. The school was shut down.

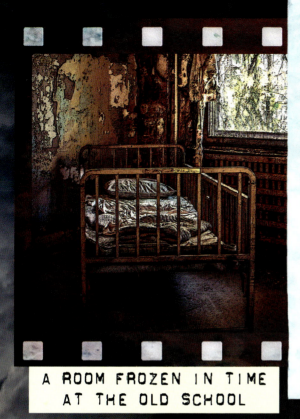

A ROOM FROZEN IN TIME AT THE OLD SCHOOL

The old school has since opened as a haunted attraction. Visitors can wander around some areas of the creepy school, left exactly as it was when it was abandoned.

Most of the attraction involves a made-up story about a brain **surgeon** doing secret experiments on prisoners in the building. The attraction is only for adults, however. It is too scary for young people!

Victoria Institution, Malaysia

The Victoria Institution is the oldest school in Kuala Lumpur, the capital of Malaysia. It was founded by the British when they ruled Malaysia, and named after Queen Victoria. The old buildings are now believed to be haunted.

During World War II, the Japanese invaded Kuala Lumpur and took over the school. Many British soldiers and local people were tortured and killed on the site.

Students have described hearing chains rattling and the eerie sound of soldiers marching. The shadow of a man has also been seen hanging from a tree in the courtyard.

THE SCHOOL PHOTOGRAPHED IN 1968

Strange things are said to have happened to some students at the school, too. Pupils have suddenly become angry and found themselves covered in mysterious bruises. The bruises disappear once the pupils become calm again.

A school band member once disappeared during a break in a late-night rehearsal. Sometime later, he was found on top of a water tank with no idea how he got there! Apparently the band member had seen a girl walking by herself and asked where she was going. The next thing he remembered was being found on the tank!

Dow Hill School, India

Two schools nestle into the wooded hills outside Kurseong in Darjeeling, India. The area is known for its beautiful views, orchid gardens, forests, and tea plantations. In India, wealthy families often send their children to school in the cool **hill stations**, as the summers get too hot in the plains and valleys. The hill station at Dow Hill has two well-known schools, Dow Hill Girls' School and Victoria Boys' School. The schools seem perfect, except they, and the nearby forest, are haunted!

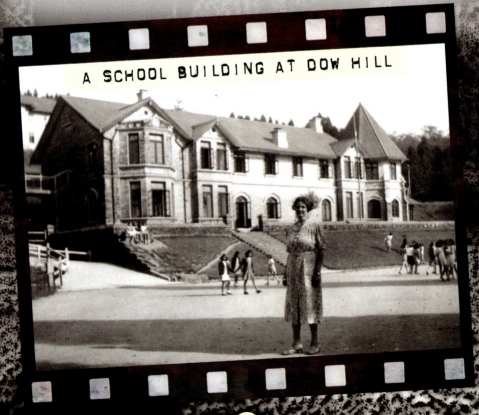
A SCHOOL BUILDING AT DOW HILL

During vacations, when the boys' school is completely empty, people have heard footsteps and laughter coming from the building. Others have seen a ghostly boy staring out of one of the windows. Both schools are next to a forest believed to be haunted. The ghost of a woman has been seen there, chasing people and uttering dreadful screams.

Glowing red eyes have been seen among the forest's trees at night!

The path that links the schools and the nearby spooky forest is known as "Death Road." Several people have seen the ghost of a headless boy walking through the trees!

William Fremd High School, Illinois

This Illinois high school is said to be haunted by several ghosts. The school auditorium is home to one **unruly** spirit, who flaps the seats up and down and plays with the theater lights. Students and teachers have experienced lights being shone onto them when the lighting control area is both empty and locked.

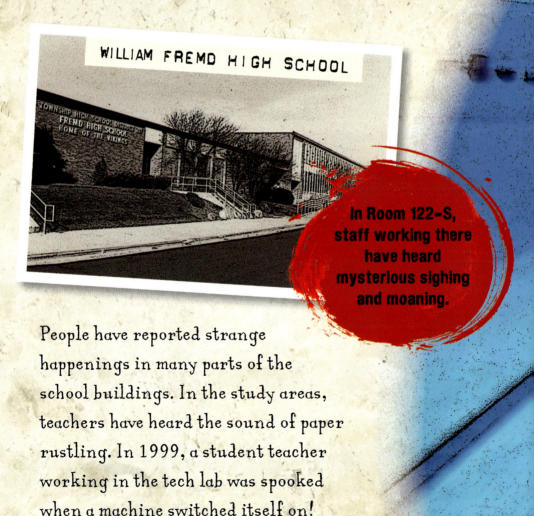

In Room 122-S, staff working there have heard mysterious sighing and moaning.

People have reported strange happenings in many parts of the school buildings. In the study areas, teachers have heard the sound of paper rustling. In 1999, a student teacher working in the tech lab was spooked when a machine switched itself on!

A terrible tragedy at the school swimming pool is behind stories of another ghost. While swimming lengths in the school pool, a freshman student suffered a heart attack and died. Since then, there have been several reports of ghostly happenings around the pool building.

A school swimsuit has been seen floating in the pool. The water near the swimsuit is said to feel ice cold, and then the suit disappears. Students say the deep end, where the girl drowned, always feels much colder than the rest of the pool. Staff members opening up the pool have also seen a strange violet haze appear over the water for a moment.

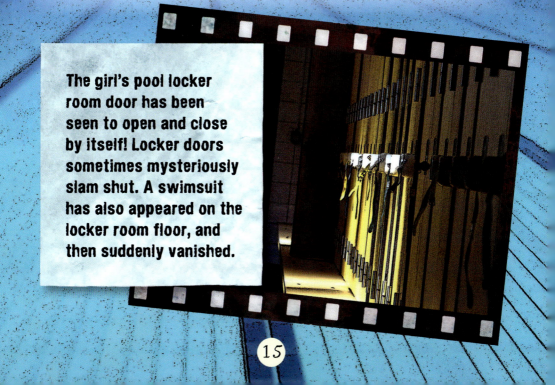

The girl's pool locker room door has been seen to open and close by itself! Locker doors sometimes mysteriously slam shut. A swimsuit has also appeared on the locker room floor, and then suddenly vanished.

Mgotjane Primary School, Swaziland

This school in Bhunya, Swaziland, Africa, has a haunted bathroom! Three girls went to the restroom one day. While one girl waited outside, the others heard a voice scream at them from one of the toilet bowls! The voice was so loud, the girl outside asked who was in there with them. Terrified, the girls ran back to class. Their teacher didn't believe them, but since then, other children have experienced the same thing.

BHUNYA, SWAZILAND

In April, 2013, a terrified teacher refused to return to the school after many sleepless nights there. She was kept awake by strange noises, and the sound of something walking on the roof. Scared, and unable to sleep, she kept the lights and TV on all night. The school was closed for several days, and community prayers were held. The police were called, but said there was nothing they could do, as the problem was caused by something **paranormal**!

Two Mgotjane teachers have reported being attacked in their rooms at night. A strange spirit tried to strangle them, or sit on their stomachs.

Yanagawa High School, Japan

In June of 2014, in a classroom at Yanagawa High School, a first-year girl suddenly started screaming, **paralyzed** in terror, unable to move. Several of her classmates started to behave in the same way. As students from nearby classes came to see what was happening, many also became **hysterical**. What caused this hysteria? No one is sure, but some believe the girls may have been possessed by a spirit.

Some time before the strange occurrence, the class had gone on a school trip to Mount Hiko and the Aburagi Dam. Both of these locations are believed to be haunted.

Mount Hiko is believed to be haunted by a headless gang on motorcycles!

THE HAUNTED DAM

The Aburagi Dam is said to be haunted by a headless schoolgirl. Could her spirit have hitched a ride with the girls when they returned to their school?

The affected girls were taken home and the school (pictured below) was closed for the following day. Experts decided that **anxiety** had caused the girls to experience a group panic attack. What do you think?

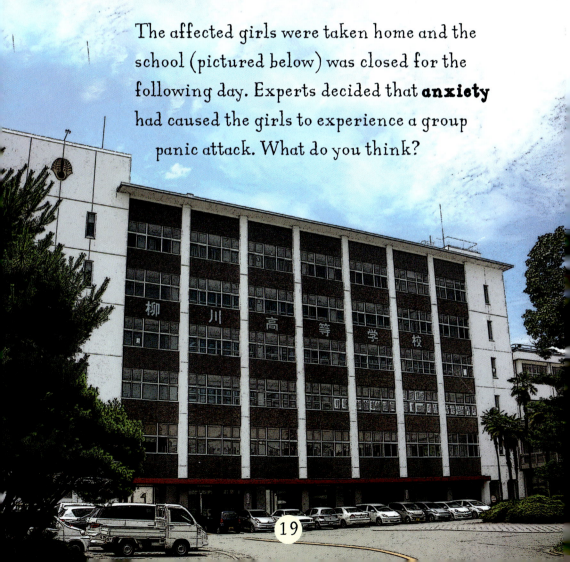

El Paso High School, Texas

El Paso High School is one of the most haunted buildings in Texas. With blocked-off classrooms frozen in time, phantom cheerleaders, a ghostly girl throwing herself from a balcony, and a spooky class photo, there is plenty to be scared about at El Paso High!

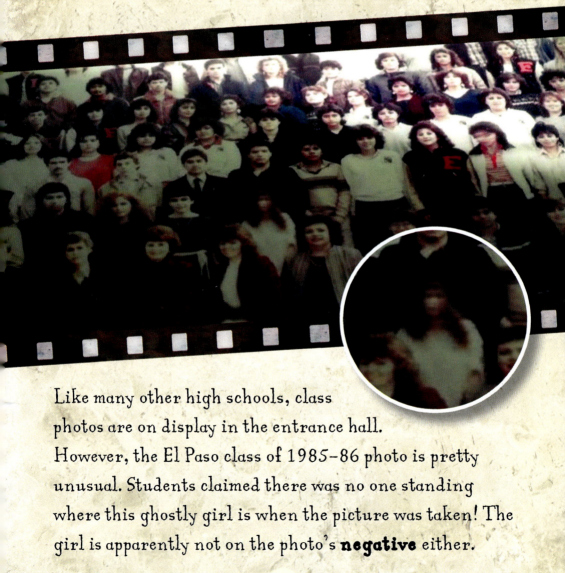

Like many other high schools, class photos are on display in the entrance hall. However, the El Paso class of 1985–86 photo is pretty unusual. Students claimed there was no one standing where this ghostly girl is when the picture was taken! The girl is apparently not on the photo's **negative** either.

One bad winter, some students and teachers got snowed in. Bored, they decided to explore a tunnel in the basement. They crawled until a wall blocked their way. Shining a flashlight through a hole made in the old bricks, they discovered a small classroom! There were antique desks, notebooks, and old candy bar wrappers on the floor.

The basement is believed to have been used to store bodies from the Spanish flu **epidemic** in the early 1900s, and also those shipped home during World War II. Could that be the reason it was blocked off?

Ghostly cheerleaders are sometimes heard singing in the empty school auditorium!

A sealed staircase leads to a haunted balcony where people claim to have seen a ghostly girl waving. Legend says a cheerleader threw herself from the balcony after breaking up with her boyfriend.

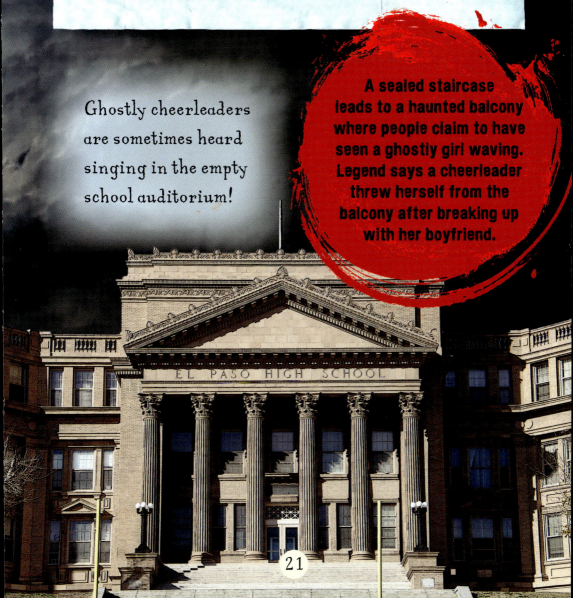

Saint Bathans' School, New Zealand

The eerie ghost town of Saint Bathans was once a busy mining town. The school was built in 1875 and quickly had to be enlarged to cope with the number of children. Suddenly, in 1899, school numbers dropped. Why? Rabbits! In the mid-1800s, rabbits were brought to New Zealand. By the late 1800s, there were thousands of them, and they were eating all the grass meant for sheep. Trapping rabbits earned good money. Children as young as six would skip school and help their families catch and skin rabbits!

THE ABANDONED SCHOOLHOUSE

By the 1940s, the school had fewer than 20 pupils. It was damaged by an earthquake in 1943. It finally closed in 1949 and the remaining seven pupils went to a nearby school. The building is now deserted. The area around the school has become home to several ghosts.

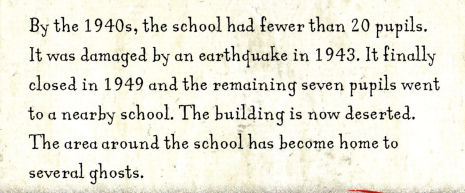

The ghost of a woman named "The Rose" is said to haunt the town's Vulcan Hotel. She was murdered in Room 1, and likes to visit and terrify male guests!

A barmaid is believed to have drowned herself in the lake created from the deep hole left by the mine workings. Long-dead miners are also thought to haunt the lake, and are seen coming out of the water late at night.

Bristol Tennessee High School, Tennessee

This high school is said to be haunted by three ghosts. The school's most famous ghost is a student known as Agnes. It is thought she died on Class Night, where the school says farewell to the seniors and welcomes the new junior class.

THE HIGH SCHOOL

Some say Agnes drowned in the school swimming pool during the Class Night party. Others say Agnes was killed when a train hit her car on a crossing on her way to the party. Students and teachers have heard ghostly footsteps and seen a spirit dressed in white wandering the corridors.

Bristol Tennessee High School is home to a most terrifying haunting! A noisy phantom train can sometimes be seen crashing along the school hallway!

Another ghost at the school is a former student who was a great athlete. He is said to have been knocked down by a car on his way home from a game. This hasn't kept him from supporting his school team. His ghost can still sometimes be seen in the school's field house on game days!

Tat Tak School, Hong Kong

Many local cab drivers refuse to take people along the road that leads to Tat Tak School. The road is lined with graves and is said to be haunted. The school itself is haunted, too, by the ghost of a woman wearing a red dress.

In Chinese culture, if someone dies wearing all red, they will return as a powerful and angry spirit. Legend has it that a teacher at the school hanged herself in the bathroom. Because she was wearing a red dress, she is believed to be a very angry ghost.

In 2001, a group of children went exploring at the abandoned school. When one of the girls saw a woman in a red dress in the graveyard, she ran screaming and warned the rest. They all ran as fast as they could. In a strange fit, the hysterical girl tried to strangle herself, and then bit a boy who tried to stop her!

ABANDONED TAT TAK SCHOOL

Other souls may be haunting Tat Tak, too. Graves of villagers killed resisting British rule have been found near the school. Also, bones of those killed by the invading Japanese were discovered nearby.

Fallsvale Elementary School, California

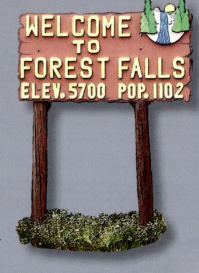

Fallsvale Elementary School in Forest Falls is surrounded by dense, spooky forest. It is also home to an abandoned old school building. If that isn't scary enough, ghostly children sometimes appear out of the trees, wanting to play with the living students! Some think the ghosts may be connected to the old two-room schoolhouse still on the site.

The boarded-up old stone school sits at the top of the drive into Fallsvale Elementary School!

The ghost children are said to like to play on the swings. People have been spooked when the swings sometimes start to move all by themselves!

Forest Falls has seen its fair share of disasters. It is one of the most dangerous places to live in California! It has suffered fires, earthquakes, floods, avalanches, mudslides, and rock falls, and is home to black bears and mountain lions.

The community takes the disasters, and the ghost children, in its stride. A local saying goes "we would rather dodge boulders than bullets," meaning they prefer the dangers of nature to those of city life.

Glossary

abandoned left empty or unused

anxiety fear or nervousness

eerie causing fear or uneasiness because of strangeness or gloominess

epidemic a rapidly spreading outbreak

epilepsy a disorder that causes attacks of convulsions, and loss of consciousness

gold rush a rapid movement of people to a newly discovered goldfield

hill station a town in the low mountains of the Indian subcontinent, popular as a resort during the hot season

hysterical suffering unmanageable fear or an outburst of emotion

negative a negative photographic image on transparent material used for printing positive pictures

paralyzed unable to act, function, or move

paranormal events beyond the scope of scientific understanding

surgeon a physician who specializes in surgery

torture to punish or force someone to do or say something by causing great pain

unruly not yielding to discipline or control

Further Information

Camisa, Kathryn. *Creepy Schools (Tiptoe into Scary Places)*. New York, NY: Bearport Publishing, 2017.

Tieck, Sarah. *Ghosts (Creepy Creatures)*. Almere, Netherlands: Buddy Books, 2015.

Website

Kidzsearch page all about ghosts
https://wiki.kidzsearch.com/wiki/ghost

Publisher's note to educators and parents: Our editors have carefully reviewed these websites to ensure that they are suitable for students. Many websites change frequently, however, and we cannot guarantee that a site's future contents will continue to meet our high standards of quality and educational value. Be advised that students should be closely supervised whenever they access the Internet.

Index

Aburagi Dam 19

Bhunya, Swaziland 16, 17
Bristol Tennessee High
 School 24, 25
Burnley Wood School 4

Dow Hill Girls' School 12, 13

El Paso High School 20, 21

Fallsville Elementary School 28, 29
Forest Falls 28, 29

Kangaroo Inn, the 6, 7
Kangaroo Inn School 6, 7

Mgotjane Primary School 16, 17
Mount Hiko 18

Pennhurst State School 8, 9

Saint Bathans 22, 23
Saint Bathans' School 22, 23

Stockport Grammar School 5

Tat Tak School 26, 27

Victoria Boys' School 12, 13
Victoria Institution 10, 11
Vulcan Hotel, Saint Bathans 23

William Fremd High School 14, 15

Yanagawa High School 18, 19

Don't be scared! Most people don't believe ghosts are real at all. No one has ever scientifically proven they exist. But it can be fun to get yourself a little spooked!